Christ's Preaching—And Ours

MICHEL PHILIBERT

JOHN KNOX PRESS

RICHMOND, VIRGINIA

Translated by Rev. David Lewis from
La Prédication de Jésus et Nous,
published by La Société Centrale
d'Evangélisation de l'Eglise Reformée de France,
Paris,
as No. 100 of *Le Revue de l'Evangélisation*, March-April 1962.

British edition by Edinburgh House Press, 1963.

American edition by John Knox Press, Richmond, Virginia, 1964.

CONTENTS

EDITORIAL PREFACE

For some time we have felt that, however widely we interpret the term 'research' for the purpose of the series of Research Pamphlets which we have been publishing since 1954, we cannot under this heading properly include a different type of study material which we are equally concerned to offer in the service of the mission of the Church. It has therefore been decided to commence a parallel series of Study Pamphlets, written on the sole responsibility of the author in each case, but selected by us in the belief that the papers thus provided offer viewpoints, challenges, and information highly stimulative of thought and study.

We have pleasure in now offering the first two numbers in this new series. This is No. 1. No. 2 is *The Relevance of Trinitarian Doctrine for Today's Mission* by Lesslie Newbigin.

The present paper is an address given to a special session of the Synod of the XIIth Region of the Reformed Church of France, held at Aix-les-Bains on February 3rd, 1962, by M. Michel Philibert, Professor of Philosophy at Grenoble.

We are grateful to Prof. Philibert for permitting us to offer these stimulating thoughts to readers in the English-speaking world. We are indebted to the Rev. David Lewis, Information Secretary of the World Presbyterian Alliance at Geneva, for his translation work. And we acknowledge with thanks the permission for this English edition granted by the Editor of *La Revue de l'Evangélisation*, Paris, in the 100th issue of which the French manuscript originally appeared.

Unless otherwise stated, biblical quotations are taken from the Revised Version, except in a few cases where they are direct translations. Careful consideration of the points raised has led us to decide that it will be more helpful to give a more or less literal rendering of the French texts from which other quotations have been taken, instead of using the official English translations.

VICTOR E. W. HAYWARD

PREFACE BY BEN L. ROSE

BECAUSE preaching is vital to the life of the Church, it must be continually re-examined. By preaching, the Church is called into being and her life nourished. Through preaching, the Church both fulfils and is enabled to fulfil her mission.

The Church cannot dispense with preaching, although there regularly arise those who suggest such a course. For God's people, there is no substitute for the proclamation of the Word of God.

Today among ordained ministers and laymen there is a healthy dissatisfaction with the Sunday sermon. The large number of books being printed on the subject indicates the Church's concern.

The appeals for a return to biblical preaching, which we have been hearing for more than a decade, have in some places strengthened the pulpit. In many other places, however, the appeals have gone unheeded, or, perhaps worse, have resulted in dull exegesis from the pulpit or in irrelevant homilies about things that occurred long ago and far away.

With the aim of causing the Church to re-examine her preaching in the light of Christ's example, this book is a significant effort toward the revitalization of the preaching ministry. Professor Philibert believes that the preaching of the New Testament, and especially of Jesus, is normative for the contemporary preacher. With diligence and insight the author examines the record of our Lord's preaching and indicates some applications of his findings for the modern Church.

The book is challenging because it does not say what everybody else is saying. The reader will hardly agree with the author at every point, but he will almost certainly be stimulated. Professor Philibert's findings threaten some current views regarding preaching. He differs with Karl Barth (or with some of Barth's followers) regarding the place of the Bible in preaching. The book performs a service in bridging the gap between the view of preaching espoused by Philipps Brooks and Charles H. Spurgeon and the view of preaching presently espoused by Karl Barth and Dietrich Ritschl.

Professor Philibert's findings also challenge some prevalent theories of counseling and of Christian education. He has done us a service by calling into question some of our cherished presuppositions.

The book does not supply simple answers. When one has finished reading it, he may ask impatiently, 'All right, professor, *how do* I make the Sunday sermon the instrument in the Church that Christ intended?' But the professor has not written a book on homiletics. He leaves the reader disturbed, and, hopefully, determined to find some answers for himself.

Certain assumptions which Professor Philibert makes about the character of French Reformed congregations cannot be made about American Protestant congregations. Instead of assuming that those to whom he preaches on Sunday morning are the faithful, the American preacher would be more correct occasionally to see the congregation before him as a field for evangelism. The wise state-side preacher does not assume that pagans do not come to church. He keeps in mind that many whose names are on the church rolls and who even attend with some regularity the services of worship have never really 'heard' the Gospel, much less believed it and committed their lives to its spread. Therefore, to employ the Sunday morning sermon exclusively as 'an instrument for the instruction of disciples' would be a mistake for American preachers.

Having said that, however, we must add that the similarity between the Continental Church and the American Church is enough for the author's applications of his findings regarding Christ's preaching to strike home to us on this side of the Atlantic.

One of the primary services which Professor Philibert renders is in emphasizing afresh that the preaching of the Church is not actually done on Sunday morning but later by the faithful who were instructed on that occasion. Thus from France comes support for Richard Niebuhr's position that the task of the ordained minister is that of pastoral director who enables the Church to fulfil its ministry. The Church is the preacher, and the function of the ordained minister is to equip the saints for the ministry of preaching.

Part One

PREACHING, TEACHING AND SERVICE

A. *Preaching as Distinct from Teaching*

THESIS I

As practised by Jesus, preaching is addressed to the people and differs in this respect from teaching, which is given to the disciples.

During the early period of his ministry Jesus travels about in Galilee teaching in synagogues and preaching the good news of the Kingdom (Mt. 4:23). Preaching and teaching are carried on side by side and sometimes intermingle (cf. Mt. 5:1 and 7:28; the Sermon on the Mount is addressed both to the crowd and to the disciples). The longer the ministry continues, however, the more marked becomes the distinction between preaching, which is addressed to all, and teaching, which is reserved for the few who have been chosen and set apart by Jesus himself. Instead of being given in public the teaching is kept private, instead of being merely unobtrusive it becomes secret. Jesus' announcement of his coming death and resurrection is not to be divulged by the disciples; and when at length they grasp the mystery of his person and mission, he insists on their keeping it to themselves.[1]

THESIS 2

Preaching and teaching do not have different themes; teaching is simply one stage between two moments of preaching.

The two different ways in which the message engages the hearer of the preaching on the one hand, and the recipient of the teaching on the other, mark two stages in their apprehension of the Gospel. In other words, they indicate which elements of the message can already be revealed to the disciple although still withheld from the hearer of the preaching.

The death and resurrection of Jesus, first announced privately and only to those already familiar with his teaching, afterwards become the central theme of the disciples' public preaching.

The precise stages gone through, from Jesus' revelation to the disciples to their transmission of it in preaching, are indicated in Acts 10:40-42. 'Him God raised up the third day, and gave him to be made manifest, not to all the people, but unto witnesses that were chosen before of God, even to us who did eat and drink with him after he rose from the dead. And he charged us to preach unto the people, and to testify that this is he which is ordained of God to be the Judge of quick and dead.'

Even before his death, Jesus' teaching revealed the mysteries of the Kingdom of God to the disciples, whereas to those 'outside' many of his deeds were like parables whose point escaped them (cf. Mk. 4:11).

This seal of secrecy placed on the teaching is only provisional, however '. . . there is nothing covered, that shall not be revealed; nor hid, that shall not be known. What I tell you in the darkness, speak ye in the light: and what ye hear in the ear, proclaim upon the housetops' (Mt. 10:26-27).

THESIS 3

Preaching is itinerant. The preacher moves forward to meet the crowds. Teaching makes the disciples move forward.

a) Jesus seeks out places and occasions where crowds assemble (synagogues, the Temple, festivals). The itinerant Jesus 'went about in all Galilee . . .' (Mt. 4:23; cf. Mt. 8:20; 9:1, 9, 27, 32, 35; 22:1).
b) When Jesus enlists the disciples in the ministry of preaching, his injunction is that they follow the same itinerant life. From this standpoint, preaching means going and announcing the Gospel to the people, going out to meet them. The itinerant disciples sent out by Jesus were the Twelve (Mt. 10:1-15; Mk. 6:7-11; Lk. 9:1-6) but also the Seventy (Lk. 10:1-12).
c) Note Jesus' call of the disciples and hearers: 'And he said to them, "Follow me!"' (Mt. 4:19; cf. 4:22, 25; 8:1, 22; Lk. 9:57-62; Mt. 10:38). The disciples are invited to leave home, work and family, to follow Jesus in his itinerant mode of life.

THESIS 4

The physical movement—of the preacher towards the people, of the disciple following the teacher—involves a social and professional uprooting. Preacher and disciple are taken out of their ordinary milieu and calling.

First there was Jesus' breach with his own family: ' . . . thy father and I have sought thee sorrowing. . . wist ye not that I must be about my Father's business?' (Lk. 2:48-9, A.V.). 'Behold my mother and my brethren' (Mt. 12:46-50). 'A prophet is not without honour, save in his own country, and among his own kin, and in his own house' (Mk. 6:1-6).

Then there was the disciples' breach with their families: ' . . . everyone that hath left houses, or brethren, or sisters, or father, or mother, or children, or lands, for my name's sake . . .' (Mt. 19:29).

Finally there was the professional and social break for both: for Jesus, the friend of publicans and sinners (cf. Lk. 7:34, 39; Mk. 2:15-17; Mt. 21:31-32), and for the disciples (Mt. 4:19, 'I will make you fishers of men').

Jesus leaves his family and district, which fail to understand his calling. He becomes difficult to place professionally. Rabbi? Prophet? Healer? Adventurer? Agitator? He gets into difficulties with the 'religious' people, both the professionals and non-professionals, and seeks out the most disreputable: the collaborators and prostitutes. To find a hearing for his message he goes anywhere, into any society.

The disciples too change their whole condition and mode of life, their livelihood and their relationships.[2]

THESIS 5

The mobility, whether physical or social and professional, which characterizes preaching and teaching, is also accompanied by a movement of the understanding, by a spiritual 'move forward'.

Jesus goes to meet the aspirations of his people. They suffer from disease and hunger, from foreign occupation and its shames. They long for dignity, deliverance, and revenge. The aspirations of the human heart (that 'den of robbers') are conflicting and changeable.

In the end every one of them will be either disappointed or amended and transformed by Jesus. He begins, however, by encouraging such aspirations, meeting them just sufficiently to strengthen them and focus them on himself. He heals the sick, feeds the multitudes, castigates collaborators, offers positions, promises glory . . .

The disciples themselves have a long spiritual road to travel before they realize that they are called to serve and not to dominate, to obey and not to lead, and that the Kingdom for which they have left all is not of this world.[3]

B. *Preaching and Teaching Are Inseparable*

THESIS 6

**The mobility which is characteristic of preaching and the mobiliza-
tion effected by teaching are linked together. The preacher moves
on, not just for the sake of future hearers, but also because this
is a means of mobilizing those who listen now.**

The preacher does not tarry. He demands an immediate decision.
Teaching takes time, involves repetition and perseverance.
Preaching is itinerant not only in the sense that it moves towards
the people, but also in the sense that it never halts but is always
moving on, outwards, elsewhere. This continued movement is
essential to preaching.

a) It is the essential condition for the universalizing of the
preaching. 'Let us go elsewhere into the next towns, that I may
preach there also; for to this end came I forth' (Mk. 1:38). '. . . and
the multitudes sought after him, and came unto him, and would
have stayed him, that he should not go from them. But he said unto
them, I must preach the good tidings of the kingdom of God to
the other cities also: for therefore was I sent' (Lk. 4:42f.). In
this sense the preacher's movement *away from* the present audience
is necessary as a movement *forwards* in order that the Gospel may
reach all.

b) The preacher's movement away from his present audience is not
just for the sake of tomorrow's audience. It is decisive for the
present hearers' salvation and essential to the authority of the
preaching. What such preaching in fact conveys is God's announcement (the Kingdom is at hand) and summons (repent!). It is not
reinforced with proofs. It is not told to engage in discussion. It
demands a decision, which is in fact the venture of faith—a decision
which is also concrete, immediate, and, if not total, yet at least
serious.

The preacher's departure presses the hearer to make the decision
demanded by the message. Anyone wanting to know more before
making a final decision must make a prior decision, namely, the
decision to make some kind of move.

Some sort of break, some acceptance of conditions, proves the faith and sincerity of anyone who expresses interest. Let him leave what he is doing and follow the preacher. On the basis of this initial obedience, discussion will be possible, and certainly there will still be many hesitations, denials and refusals to be experienced before the disciple gets in the clear. But he must take a first step, he must begin to move. 'One thing thou lackest; go, sell whatsoever thou hast, and give to the poor, and thou shalt have treasure in heaven: and come, follow me' (Mk. 10: 17-21). This is what Jesus says to the rich young man he loved. It is not a sacrifice he is demanding, but a deliverance he is offering, so that this young man may be in a position to receive a gift, namely, that understanding of the mysteries of the Kingdom of God which many prophets and righteous men desired to see, yet in vain. 'Blessed are your eyes, for they see,' says Jesus to his disciples—to those who had followed him (Mt. 13: 16-17).

The first step, the first thing to be done, is to follow the teaching. This means in fact following the teacher. 'If any man willeth to do his will, he shall know of the teaching, whether it be of God' (Jn. 7: 17). This step must be taken today. 'Behold, I set before you the way of life and the way of death' (Jer. 21:8). The preacher cannot allow his hearer to assume that he can postpone his decision to a time more convenient to himself. The hearer must not be led into temptation to settle down into a permanent and fatal procrastination. That is why the preacher must not tarry, but be on his way.

The hearer's departure in the wake of the preacher he has accepted as his teacher expresses in concrete fashion his repentance, his conversion, his abandonment of the past. The disciple will leave the dead to bury the dead. He will not renounce Sin as an abstract concept, but as a way of living, a system of habits, an image of himself proposed to him by others, in which they shut him up. There is restored to him a freedom to grow beyond the bounds he thought possible while he was still a prisoner of his own past and of other people's ideas of him.

The preacher's movement away from his present audience is

intended, not so much to separate him from it, as rather to draw those of its members awakened by the preaching away from the setting which held them prisoner. This constitutes the difference between those who obey and those who ignore the summons. The preacher's departure, which conditions the disciple's departure, provides for him and for others a test of his real concern.[4]

THESIS 7

Thus the decision for the Gospel claimed by preaching is expressed concretely, first of all, in an immediate decision to depart and to follow the teaching. This break is a sign and a condition of the disciple's readiness for continued growth and renewal.

The aim of teaching is not to announce God's decision and to call for man's decision, as in the case of preaching. It is to make a new man of the disciple and enrol him in a team, this enrolment being itself, moreover, one of the means to his renewal. The disciple's emotional attitudes, behaviour, and understanding need re-education. He must be given new standards. Care must be taken over his growth and development. This is a slow process, calling for much patience, and effective only in small groups. It calls for intimacy, for the sharing of tasks and responsibilities, of risks and hopes, of joys and sorrows, for shared effort and shared relaxation, for common worship and prayer together. A break with the old circle and its customs, with the character shaped and shut in by it, is demanded if the new man is to be born, grow and develop.[5]

THESIS 8

The new birth must be followed by new growth. For this, study, knowledge, and the continued renewal of understanding are essential.

I have pointed out elsewhere[6] that Jesus' summons to become as little children (Mt. 18:3), to be born again (Jn. 3:3), is not contradicted by the exhortation of Paul and the Epistles to become mature in judgment (I Cor. 14:20), no longer to think as children but to put away 'childish things', to leave behind the breast-feeding stage and to go on to solid food (I Cor. 3: 1f.; Heb. 5: 11-14). Both these summonses are invitations to start growing again, to remember that, from the spiritual standpoint, we do not attain maturity by a natural process. We have not arrived, not finished growing, thank God. We are not able to live from now on by what we have already acquired, needing to make no more progress. We are not complete and mature beings, fully grown and established, which would really mean being dead folk who happen to be still existing! Being 'adult', if this were the sense, would mean remaining at a lower stage of development than God intended for us, inasmuch as complacency, pride and vanity stopped our growth and arrested our development.

Jesus Christ delivers us from this illusion and its paralysing effects. He invites us to think of ourselves not as having arrived at maturity, but as needing to become as children who want to grow up and who do in fact grow up to resemble their parents. 'Become as children!' says Jesus. 'In order to become grown up!' explains Paul. Peter, too, stresses that the new birth is followed by new growth: 'As newborn babes, long for the spiritual milk which is without guile, that ye may grow thereby unto salvation' (I Peter 2:2).

Clearly then, in this spiritual growth to which Christ summons us, knowledge is a vital element, an indispensable ingredient. 'We increase by the knowledge of God' (Col. 1:10, R.V. margin).[7] 'And having put on the new man, which is being renewed unto knowledge after the image of him that created him' (Col. 3:10).

According to a very ancient idea, already popular among the Greeks and adopted by Paul, the process of knowing produces a change in the very nature of the knowing subject, with the result that he becomes like the object known. We still speak of 'assimilating' knowledge, implying by this metaphor, taken from the digestive process, that the mind makes its own what it learns and transforms it into its own substance. Assimilation is here used in a sense opposite to that emphasized in antiquity. By incorporating the thing or being known into itself, the spirit and the whole person come to resemble it. Some very recent theories have taken up these ideas. In psycho-analysis for example, Lacan, following the views of Charlotte Buhler, represents the subject's development as a series of ideal identifications. He locates the basis of psychic causality in the subject's attraction to an image of itself into which it projects itself and with which it identifies itself by interiorizing the image.

A simpler illustration is provided by our own observation of ordinary life. We notice sometimes how an elderly married couple gradually come to resemble each other as a result of having lived together for many years, or how adopted children come in time to develop a physical resemblance to their adoptive parents. This may help us to understand the expression used by Paul, for example, when he says, '. . . we all, with unveiled face reflecting as a mirror the glory of the Lord, are transformed into the same image from glory to glory, even as from the Lord the Spirit' (II Cor. 3:18).

This helps us to understand why it was essential for those hearers who wished to be formed and to grow into likeness to Christ to follow him so as to receive his teaching. They needed not only verbal instruction but also to be taught by his example and by sharing his life. So, too, it has been essential, since his ascension, to contemplate his image in the clear mirror of the Gospel, yet also to follow and share his life in the life of the humble, the 'least', the poor, the hungry and the prisoners. It is in fact his image which releases, guides and nourishes our growth towards full human stature. Just as a plant in a dark room turns and grows towards the window through which the light and life stream, so too the light and life of Christ enable us to grow. Only after becoming Christ-oriented can we become 'Christophers', Christ-bearers. Paul affirmed that this growth continues in the Christian and in the Church: 'Till we all attain unto the unity of the faith, and of the knowledge of the Son of God, unto a fullgrown man, unto the measure of the stature of the fulness of Christ: that we may be no longer children, tossed to and fro and carried about with every wind of doctrine, by the sleight of men, in craftiness, after the wiles of error; but speaking truth in love, may grow up in all things into him, which is the head, even Christ; from whom all the body fitly framed and knit together through that which every joint supplieth, according to the working in due measure of each several part, maketh the increase of the body unto the building up of itself in love' (Eph. 4).

Our understanding is at once the beneficiary and, under the action of grace, also the agent of this transformation, this constant renewal, this continuing growth of our inner being, which, according to II Cor. 4:16, is being renewed day by day. We are to be transformed by the renewal of our mind, in order that we may discern the good and acceptable and perfect will of God (Rom. 12:2).

C. *Preaching and Service Are Inseparable*

THESIS 9

Works accompany preaching from the beginning. The significance of Jesus' works is more important than their effect. Service is a facet and illustration of preaching.

We must now introduce into our analysis of preaching an element which has so far, for convenience, been omitted, but which is clearly related to preaching, namely service.

We read in Mt. 4:23 that 'Jesus went about in all Galilee, teaching in their synagogues and preaching the gospel of the kingdom, and healing all manner of disease and all manner of sickness among the people.' Healing is associated with preaching and teaching.[8] The same association is found in Titus 2: 6-8: 'The younger men likewise exhort to be soberminded: in all things shewing thyself an example of good works; in thy doctrine shewing uncorruptness, gravity, sound speech that cannot be condemned.'

According to the Sermon on the Mount, testimony (preaching) illuminates works so as to bring out their meaning. 'Ye are the light of the world . . . let your light shine before men, that they may see your good works, and glorify your Father which is in heaven' (Mt. 5:14-16). So too in I Pet. 2:12: 'Having your behaviour seemly among the Gentiles; that, wherein they speak against you as evil-doers, they may by your good works, which they behold, glorify God in the day of visitation.' It 'is the will of God, that by well-doing ye should put to silence the ignorance of foolish men' (v. 15).

This connection between action and witness appears again in II Cor. 9, where Paul, when asking help for the brethren, says: ' . . . the ministration of this service not only filleth up the measure of the wants of the saints, but aboundeth also through many thanksgivings unto God; seeing that through the proving of you by this ministration they glorify God for the obedience of *your confession unto the gospel of Christ, and for the liberality of your contribution* unto them and unto all' (v. 12f.).

(An objection might be raised from Mt. 6:1: 'Take heed that ye do not your righteousness before men, to be seen of them: else ye have no reward with your Father which is in heaven.' This injunction to secrecy in almsgiving and fasting seems to condemn not merely the motive of pride, but also the open, public practice of them. But later in the Sermon, Mt. 7:15-20, it is said that prophets are like trees, known by their good or bad fruit, and a distinction is made between doing the Father's will and mere lip-service (vv. 21-27).)

The healing of the paralytic is presented as intended to illustrate the preaching. According to Mk. 2:1-12, the service rendered to the paralytic is a means rather than an end: 'But that ye may know that the Son of man hath power on earth to forgive sins . . . I say unto thee [he said to the paralytic] arise.'

This brings us to consider the 'miracles' of Jesus. The term 'miracle' and the scientific controversies to which it has given rise have stressed the idea of a breach of natural laws, indicating Jesus' authority over creation. Such an emphasis tends to make us overlook the idea of 'admiration' or 'wonder' which the word 'miracle' contains (mirari—to be astonished at), and which directs attention not so much to a breach of objective natural laws as to a breach with our ordinary ways of thinking. A 'miracle' is primarily an astonishing act which attracts and holds our attention by breaking through the customary and the ordinary. This comes closer to the meaning of the Greek word sēmeion which is translated sometimes by 'miracle', sometimes by 'sign'. The miracle, the service rendered, is a sign. It does not simply carry out a desire to serve and to render a benefit; it signalizes that desire, indicates it, translates it, publishes it.

Jesus washed the feet of his disciples. This was a very concrete act, a very material service, which we might well say 'spoke louder than words'. But what was intended by it was not primarily the cleansing of the disciples or their comfort. Its unusual character was intended to strike the imagination of the disciples, and to lead them to reflect on the hidden significance of such an act. By withholding the explanation, Jesus keeps them in suspense and stimulates their curiosity: 'What I do thou knowest not now; but thou shalt understand hereafter' (Jn. 13:7). In fact Jesus was giving them an example to illustrate a command. This example points to a more important service and sacrifice than the washing of the disciples' feet, and the command it illustrates enjoins on the Christian a more costly and continuing service than mere washing.

This does not mean that the acts of service and love which, following Christ's example, the disciples are called upon to perform are not motivated by concern for the neighbour's good. Yet we must not overlook the special importance of this episode.

Neither Christ's service nor that of Christians is aimed directly and immediately at eliminating all the sufferings which burden the human race. It was in fact by a much more radical and complete gift, yet one whose final and ultimate effect is deferred, namely by the gift of his life, that Christ bore our griefs and delivered us from their dominion. The sole purpose which the Christian can assign to his service, to his works, is that they should point to Christ's sacrifice, Christ's love and Christ's kingdom. That is why it is wholly appropriate for them to have a very special character.

What we have said in no way belittles the value of devoted and sacrificial acts on the part of believers, as of non-believers, when done in a spirit of love, whether quietly and secretly without witnesses other than their beneficiaries, or whether, as at times, witnessed only by God. Wherever such acts are done, even though unbeknown to men and though without any reference to Christian faith, we know that Christ is their hidden beneficiary and the Spirit their hidden inspirer. But wherever such works are to be seen, it is for the Christian to discern and proclaim those which are signs of the age to come in the midst of this passing age, whoever may be their authors, even if they are strangers to the faith. The Christian must discern what is conformed to the good and acceptable and perfect will of God, and praise God for it. In such acts God reveals himself as the Lord even of those who do not know his name or who reject his commands, while some Christians who call him Lord withhold obedience from him.

None the less, as Christ's ambassadors we are still required to show by manifest signs that we belong to our Master. We are still required to make a decisive break with certain habitual ways characteristic of our environment, not to be conformed to the elements of this passing age, to be nonconformists. This means that we are required to seek the extraordinary. 'What do ye more than others?' What are you doing which contrasts so strikingly with the ways of non-believers that they are compelled to ask why you behave in so inexplicable a fashion? Because of this the Christian's service will always find expression more naturally in events than in institutions. Though a total giving is required, it is for a service which cannot but be incomplete and provisional in comparison with actual material needs, a service which will have served its purpose if its significance is perceived.

The parable of the good Samaritan serves only to underline the unpredictable, improvised, circumstantial character of the service for which the providential hazards of the journey provide the opportunities. Need we remind those who speak frequently of serving the neighbour, and who identify this 'neighbour' with the person 'next to us', the man next door, the acquaintance, that it was on the road that the Samaritan encountered the man he went to help, and that we too are called to be wayfarers, spiritually and literally, if we are to be what in fact we are, 'strangers and pilgrims on the earth'?

Service thus illustrates preaching, and preaching illuminates service. Just as the electric light flashes between two poles, so the light of Christ flashes between the pole of the Word and the pole of the Act, and illuminates both together. Neither the Word alone without the Act, nor the Act alone without the meaning given it by the spoken witness, can claim to cause the spark of grace to flash out, the flame of the Spirit to come down, to illuminate our darkness and set our hearts on fire.

Anticipating Theses 12 and 13, we may say that sacrifice constitutes the essential unity between preaching and service. The theme of preaching is the service and sacrifice offered by Christ; the effect of preaching is the service and sacrifice offered by the disciple.

THESIS 10

The preaching of Jesus unfolded; it was nourished by the circumstances it encountered and by the response made to it.

The preaching of Jesus unfolded and developed. At first it was no different from that of John the Baptist: 'Repent ye; for the kingdom of heaven is at hand.' But gradually a difference emerges, a new note is heard, an authority is asserted. The teaching of Jesus breaks with the traditional teaching ('It was said to them of old time . . . but I say unto you . . .'), with John's teaching (who came neither eating nor drinking), and with that of the Pharisees and Sadducees, of whom the disciples must beware as of bad leaven. New in tone and content, impressive from the very outset ('as one having authority and not as their scribes'), the teaching of Jesus advances and deepens as his ministry continues. He teaches his disciples new things, new in relation to his initial teaching, that is, things so astonishing that at first they fail to understand them. 'From that time began Jesus to shew unto his disciples, how that he must go unto Jerusalem, and suffer many things . . . and be killed, and the third day be raised again.'

His preaching made use of the circumstances he encountered and fastened on the responses made to it. Though continuing to preach to the crowds and to teach the disciples privately, Jesus still had private meetings and public meetings with wayfarers, questioners, sympathizers and enemies. Some of these meetings were in the presence of disciples or before a crowd. Even when the crowd remained silent, it was not merely a witness, not simply a background, but often the real audience and in a sense the arbiter of the encounter.

We need to stress the extent to which the actions, agreements and questionings of his hearers, in so far as they were called forth by Jesus' preaching, were taken up into his teaching. A good deal of the Master's teaching consists of responses to circumstances: the centurion's faith, the scribe's zeal, the hesitancy of the would-be disciple in mourning, the unbelief of the Twelve, the Baptist's question from prison, the obstinacy of Bethsaida and Chorazin, the criticisms and trap questions of the Pharisees, the aimlessness of the multitude, these are a few of the many instances on which the occasion furnished Jesus with opportunities for teaching, and even in part determined its content.

Taken as a whole and in its mode of development, Jesus' preaching not only evokes but also makes use of the response of those to whom it is directed. The parable of the wicked husbandmen shows how Jesus' preaching combines an undeviating and reiterated purpose (to receive the fruits of the vineyard) with a resourcefulness which is always adapted to the response last received (they will reverence my son) and an announcement of the necessary changes involved (the kingdom shall be taken away from you and given to a nation bringing forth the fruits thereof).

THESIS 11

The preaching of Jesus showed a development. At its deepest, it centred upon his death, the penalty of his apparent human failure turned into the instrument of his victory.

The analysis in Thesis 10, indicating the connection between preaching and the circumstances it encountered or provoked and then utilized, was still only in terms of its form. Turning now to the content of this preaching, we see that, as it developed, it was in fact increasingly concerned with the person, and finally with the death, of its author, himself its essential theme. The proclamation of the Kingdom becomes a pointing out of the only door giving access to it, the only way leading to it, a proclamation of the King to whom the Father has given his own authority and power.[9]

The condemnation to death of the preacher Jesus expresses—to say the least—the unbelief of his hearers. It comes about because of their refusal to obey, and it sets a seal on this refusal. It thus indicates the failure of preaching to reach and convert all those who had heard it. Yet Jesus, who anticipated his condemnation, did not regard it as a misfortune which would put an end to preaching, as an obstacle to be avoided at all costs. He held and taught that his death was necessary. 'Behoved it not the Christ to suffer all these things and to enter into his glory?' He consented to his death and even willed it. 'No man taketh my life from me. I lay it down of myself.' It was necessary for the salvation of others, for the salvation of all. Instead of being an obstacle to the continuance of his preaching, a bar to its universal extension, Jesus made it the means to assert this universality, to ensure this continuance. His death marked the transition from his own direct preaching to a preaching mediated by his disciples, that is, of which the disciples were the means, transmitted by them as intermediaries. It was his death which made their preaching effective. Death did not mean the end of Jesus' mission but rather the unavoidable detour which enabled him to reach the goal envisaged from the very beginning. 'The bread which I will give is my flesh *for the life of the world.*' Or, again, and this other Johannine formula states exactly how Jesus' death, apparently the final obstacle to the universalizing of his preaching, becomes instead the means of its realization: 'I, if I be lifted up from the earth, will draw all men unto myself. But this he said, signifying by what manner of death he should die' (Jn. 12:32f.).

To transform an obstacle into an instrument is normally a work of art, the skilful stratagem of a creator. If the obstacle in question is death, the operation calls for the omnipotence of the Sovereign Creator!

THESIS 12

Persecution accompanies preaching, as its shadow.

To some extent every light casts shadows, and the light of revelation is no exception. 'The light is come into the world, and men loved the darkness rather than the light; for their works were evil' (Jn. 3:19). One hesitates to formulate this thesis, though it is along the same line as the previous thesis. Does it not suggest despair of human nature and of God's grace? Certainly one would not be justified in venturing to state it *a priori.* Jesus himself did not despair of the response he would receive. He makes the owner of the vineyard say: 'They will reverence my son.' That is to say, he did not undertake his mission without hope. Nor did the lack of immediate success prevent him from going forward with perseverance: 'O Jerusalem, Jerusalem, which killeth the prophets, and stoneth them that are sent unto her! how often would I have gathered thy children together, even as a hen gathereth her chickens under her wings, and ye would not' (Mt. 23:37).

Yet elsewhere it was not so much unbelief which astonished him ('he marvelled at their unbelief') as faith. 'And when Jesus heard it, he marvelled, and said to them that followed, Verily I say unto you, I have not found so great faith, no, not in Israel' (Mt. 8:10). Jesus was prepared to see his preaching cause trouble and provoke anger. Indeed he regarded this as part of his mission. Because it demanded decision, his preaching would meet refusal as well as acceptance, hostility as well as obedience.[10] 'Think not that I came to send peace on the earth: I came not to send peace, but a sword. For I came to set a man at variance against his father, and the daughter against her mother, and the daughter in law against her mother in law' (Mt. 10: 34-35).

In the light of what happened, the persecution which the preaching provoked, as an attempt at suppression, is seen as necessary for the attainment of the end which preaching has in view. 'And he began to teach them, that the Son of man must suffer many things, and be rejected by the elders, and the chief priests and the scribes, and be killed, and after three days rise again' (Mk. 8:31).

What applies to the Master applies also to the disciples. 'It is enough for the disciple that he be as his master, and the servant as his lord. If they have called the master of the house Beelzebub, how much more shall they call them of his own household! . . . he that doth not take his cross and follow after me, is not worthy of me' (Mt. 10: 25, 38).[11]

Jesus also sent his disciples out on a mission 'as sheep in the midst of wolves' and warned them what they were to expect: 'But beware of men: for they will deliver you up to councils, and in their synagogues they will scourge you; yea and before governors and kings shall ye be brought for my sake' (Mt. 10: 17-18). 'And ye shall be hated of all men for my name's sake' (v. 22). (Cf. G. Bernanos in *Diary of a Country Priest:* 'The true priest is never loved.')

According to the teaching of Jesus, persecution has several effects or, as one might even say, purposes.

It tests a person's faith. 'And ye shall be hated of all men for my name's sake: but he that endureth to the end, the same shall be saved' (Mt. 10:22). It is right to pray to be delivered from temptation in this sense. In the Lord's Prayer, Jesus teaches us to pray, 'Lead us not into temptation,' and in Gethsemane, he himself prayed, 'If it be possible, let this cup pass from me.' When temptation comes, however, we are to receive it as a grace which is meant to confirm our calling. 'Blessed are ye, when men shall hate you, and when they shall separate you from their company, and reproach you, and cast out your name as evil, for the Son of man's sake. Rejoice in that day, and leap for joy: for behold, your reward is great in heaven: for in the same manner did their fathers unto the prophets' (Lk. 6: 22f.). 'There is no man that hath left house, or brethren, or sisters, or mother, or father, or children, or lands, for my sake, and for the gospel's sake, but he shall receive a hundredfold now in this time, houses, and brethren, and sisters, and mothers, and children, and lands, with persecutions; and in the world to come eternal life' (Mk. 10: 29-30). We may accept persecution with trust and confidence, remembering how Jesus prayed for Simon that when he was sifted by Satan, his faith would not fail (Lk. 22: 31-32), and trusting in the promise of the immediate and timely help of the Holy Spirit (Mt. 10: 19-20).

Persecution provides opportunity for witnessing to the faith. Its purpose is therefore apostolic. 'Yea and before governors and kings shall ye be brought for my sake, for a testimony to them and to the Gentiles' (Mt. 10: 18).

Persecution maintains the itinerant movement of preaching and, by accelerating its spread throughout the world, it hastens the return of Christ. 'But when they persecute you in this city, flee into the next: for verily I say unto you, Ye shall not have gone through the cities of Israel, till the Son of man be come' (Mt. 10: 23). Therefore it is perhaps not so much a delay of Christ's return which obliges the Church to settle down in the world, as stagnation in the Church which delays Christ's return.

The Acts of the Apostles abundantly illustrates how these warnings of Christ were confirmed in experience.

When the Spirit blows, there is a noise, the multitude hurries to the spot, all are astonished, and some mock (Acts 2). When the apostles teach the people in the Temple porticos, the officials intervene and imprison them. They are brought before the courts, thus being given a fresh opportunity to bear witness in public. Their disobedience to the order to cease preaching and teaching in the name of Jesus provokes fresh persecution; and we are told that, after being beaten with rods, the apostles 'departed from the presence of the council, rejoicing that they were counted worthy to suffer dishonour for the name' (Acts 5:41).

To these testimonies we add two comments. The first is by Kierkegaard in his *Le droit de mourir pour la vérité*: 'Of all the nonsense uttered in these miserable times, perhaps the most nonsensical is the sentence, written with a pretence to wisdom which I have often enough met with in the course of my reading and whose excellence I have also heard some people praise: "Nowadays no man can be a martyr any more, for ours is an age incapable of making a martyr of anyone." What a misconception! We are not to think it is the age which has the power to put a man to death or to make him a martyr. It is the martyr, the genuine martyr, who must give to the age the passion, the bitter passion to want to kill him . . . Real superiority always works in two ways: it produces the force which brings about its own fall. Thus when a disturber of consciences is to be put to death, it is not the age which in its own strength leads him to the gallows, but he himself who, by dealing his salutary blows, gives to the age the passionate desire to kill him. And, if the age is sunk in the worst kind of laxity, such a brave man has only to appear to disturb it to the core.' But the whole of this short work should be pondered.[12]

Next E. Mathiot, who writes in *Simples remarques sur la prédication* (Cahiers Protestants 1960, No. 1. and La Confiance 1961, No. 3): 'I am still appalled by all the fine words I have uttered from the pulpit Sunday by Sunday for twenty-five years, any one of which lived out up to the hilt would have been enough to send me to prison. If Christianity is not persecuted in the West, it owes its relative security to its infidelity. God's blessing is withdrawn and cannot be experienced in the midst of our verbal sonorities. It seeks a truly adventuring life . . . God gives to us only by halves because we trust him only by halves.'

D. *Teaching Created by and for Preaching*

THESIS 13

Teaching directly associates the disciples with the task of preaching. Their participation in preaching is one of the ways by which they receive instruction.

The disciple is as receptive to teaching as any hearer is to preaching. The disciple differs from the hearer of preaching in being actively enlisted for the task of preaching. Having once set out after the Teacher, he is not one who only waits for further instruction, but one who passes the message on and is sent out by Jesus so to do. It appears that Jesus on more than one occasion sent the disciples out on temporary preaching missions. What the disciple has heard in secret he proclaims from the roof-top. In other words, he is no longer one of the crowd being taught by Jesus, he is at Jesus' side helping him teach the crowd.

This participation of the disciple in the work of preaching is from the very beginning one of the means of his own instruction. We need to stress in this connection the fact that the disciples are hardly ready for these immediate impromptu missions. When Jesus sends them out, though they have made their decision to follow him and have had the benefit of initial instruction, they are far from comprehending the meaning of the venture on which they are embarked, far from mastering its intricacies or being able to forecast its end. As to the Kingdom the imminence of which Jesus has affirmed, and which he commands them to proclaim, they do not as yet grasp its dimensions, its laws, or who will inherit it. Long after these preaching missions we have evidence of their failure to comprehend, of their disobedience, confusion, and disorder. In other words, Jesus did not wait until they were fully instructed before entrusting them with the work of preaching.

In fact, no great intellectual training, no exceptional skill in speech, nor even complete understanding of the message to be delivered, is required for the announcing of an event or the carrying of a message—only a faithful transmission. Neither unusual powers, nor superhuman perfection, nor remarkable piety is called for here.

An initial and minimal understanding of the message, plus an awareness of the importance attached by the Lord Jesus to its delivery, is sufficient for its perception by those for whom it is intended. It is thus easy to see why preaching *can* be entrusted to men who are not intellectuals or scholars, or even confirmed in their faith.[13]

It can and should be entrusted to such, because preaching is one of the ways by which the disciple can express his obedience concretely. It is an indispensable condition, both for continuing to receive instruction and also for growth in understanding, in accordance with the principle—already referred to above—of the correlation between doing and knowing. ('If any man willeth to do his will, he shall know of the teaching, whether it be of God' Jn. 7:17.) A second principle, that of the correlation between impression and expression explains how the preaching engaged in by the disciples provides them with an opportunity for their own growth. We know really well only something which we have to teach. We never learn or understand anything so well as that which we have to formulate and explain to others. We have deep and lasting impressions only of things we have expressed. In preaching to others, the disciple himself is strengthened. Since to dare to say even a little, we need to know more ('out of the abundance of the heart, the mouth speaketh'), the obligation to preach stimulates and fortifies the will to learn.

Knowledge which we keep to ourselves remains sterile even for ourselves. We appear to take it in, but unless there is a deliberate effort to express it, it does not remain. We take it into our minds, yet we can keep it inwardly at a distance and have reservations and doubts about it. To pass it on compels us to make it really our own. The failure of others to understand it, their objections to it, which we recognize as echoes of our own failures to understand and of our own objections, compel us to clarify it for ourselves, to go deeper, and to turn again and again to the Master himself.

The joy of having been heard and understood strengthens us more and more, the first successes encourage us, provided we are given the opportunity of taking stock of our efforts, of voicing our reactions, of assessing the results. Jesus makes use of this, too, as a means of instruction: 'And the seventy returned with joy, saying, Lord, even the devils are subject to us in thy name. And he said unto them [how heartening!], I beheld Satan fallen as lightning from heaven.' He goes on to confirm them in their mission and authority: 'Behold, I have given you authority to tread upon serpents and scorpions, and over all the power of the enemy.' Finally, he reminds them of the essential thing: 'Howbeit in this rejoice not, that the spirits are subject unto you; but rejoice that your names are written in heaven' (Lk. 10: 17-20).

Finally, as has already been indicated and will be repeated later on, the persecution which accompanies it also helps to make preaching a means of instructing the disciples.

Thus we reap benefit from the Gospel only as we pass it on. That is why, in the practice of Jesus, passing the message on is not something subsequent or extrinsic to instruction in the faith, but an essential element of the instruction itself.

THESIS 14

Sharing in the work of preaching is not merely a means of instructing the disciples in the faith, it is also the purpose of this instruction. The disciples will have to continue the preaching.

The teaching given to the few has as its purpose the preaching intended for all. Too many people in too vast a world make it impossible for Jesus, in one too short life, to reach all men everywhere directly with his voice. Moreover the very vigour of his preaching will provoke the reactions that will bring it to an end. To carry his salvation to all, Jesus had to establish a community, not only to assist him in the task of his own lifetime, but also to survive him, to succeed him, and to continue his work. Teaching is a means to an end. It is the training of the disciples, making a Church out of those whose purpose is to preach and teach the Gospel to all the nations. The ultimate purpose of the teaching given to the disciples is the preaching of the whole Church to all men.

The teaching thus appears, now as the purpose, now as the means, of the preaching. Preaching invites the hearer to become a disciple, to follow Jesus and his teaching. Teaching prepares the disciple for mission. He is to pass the message on and continue the preaching.

To 'continue' it—not merely to listen and then repeat, but better still to continue, his Master's preaching and teaching. It is important to insist on this point.

THESIS 15

To hand on his message, Jesus left behind him not writings but disciples.

The method to which modern men immediately turn, in order to ensure the survival of their message after they are dead, is writing. Writing enables us to extend communication beyond the present limits of time and space. It removes the barriers which check the sound of the spoken word. It also offers the hope of compensation for present failures. What my neighbours fail to understand, others farther afield may perhaps grasp. What my contemporaries reject, their children or grandchildren will one day accept. The author of a written and published work which meets with no general acceptance now may yet hope for an unending succession of favourable responses in the future. The unlimited series of the generations to come represents for him a substitute for immediate success, for the universality inaccessible to him today.

Writing offers a possibility, but also a danger; a temptation as well as a hope. The danger is of evading the difficulties of communication in the present, in pursuit of a future, deferred and indirect communication. The latter is no doubt easier, but it is also poorer; unlimited perhaps, but also diluted, like a drop of water in the ocean. Relying on the hope of future success, I no longer venture all my resources in today's encounter. To persuade this man is hard work, to contradict that man is dangerous. What is the point of breaking my head against their stupidity, ambition and hostility? Some fine day posterity will vindicate me. I will bide my time, be patient, husband my resources. In other words, I cheat my contemporaries, desert and abandon them.

Again, however attentively the reader engages in a silent dialogue with the written work, which gradually changes both the reader, deeply influenced by the work, and the work's meaning for him, whether by enrichment or distortion—however many twists and turns may occur in the long career of a once-published work, with its succession of different publics—it yet remains true that the writer's work ends with publication. Whatever fruits of earlier encounters may have gone into the work, whatever anticipations it may contain of the reaction of future readers, publication inevitably brings to an end something of the reciprocity of communication. What I have written, I have written. It can no longer be nourished by the other person's response.

Jesus' consciousness of the inevitable suspicion and mistrust encountered by a prophet in his own country does not deflect him from his present duty. 'I was not sent but unto the lost sheep of the house of Israel' (Mt. 15: 24). So it was with Socrates. He believed that he was divinely sent to Athens to arouse and rebuke his fellow-citizens, but never to abandon them. So he neglected his own interests for theirs. He preferred death to the exile or voluntary silence which would have deprived them of his message. Both Jesus and Socrates put everything they had into their spoken words, into the present encounter with their fellow-citizens and contemporaries, then and there.

Jesus left men behind him, not writings. A Latin author, aware of the difficulties which family responsibilities place in the way of writing books, once said it was necessary to choose between producing a family and producing books. '*Aut liberi, aut libri!*' Jesus refused the escape-hatch of writing books. He chose instead to beget children. He did not print pages but imprinted hearts. He did not write gospels, but inspired evangelists instead. The writing and production of books is a difficult art. It is an even more difficult art, and a much rarer and more sublime art, to produce writers. Jesus did not imprison his thought and influence in writings, giving his message a written, definitive form. Rather, he left in hearts and minds so deep an impression that it could not but find expression in time in the writings of others, of those who came to receive his message.

Another Latin proverb contrasts the vanity of the spoken word with the gravity and efficacy of the written word: *'verba volant, scripta manent'* (words fly away, but writings remain). Here, too, Jesus turns our customary ideas upside down. My words, he says, will never pass away.

Only rarely do we take the risk of training disciples. Cowardice, pride, and vanity probably explain our hesitation as much as does modesty. We always imagine that disciples would misrepresent our message, and so we prefer to write. It may be that our distrust of our hearers contributes to their reluctance to trust us, and so induces the very thing it fears. Why should they trust us, when we ourselves stop short of such complete trust, by taking out an insurance against them in favour of posterity?

Jesus risked all—the future of his message, the salvation of the generations to come—on a handful of men on whom he had worked for two or three short years.

Jesus left behind him, not a book for them to reproduce verbatim, but a Spirit who would lead them into all truth.

Their encounter with the King put them into the position of being able to bring out of their treasury things new and old. By royal warrant, they had a licence to print money!

To meet the needs of the disciples whom they in turn would make, they did not require to keep returning to the same place, in order, like the Danaïdes in Greek mythology, to draw water with leaking pitchers. They had within themselves a well of water springing up into eternal life.

Rooted in Christ, they also grew and waxed strong in him. The deeper their roots went, the higher their branches, the more abundant their fruit.

E. *Conclusions*

THESIS 16

Preaching begins with the known so as to lead the hearer to the unknown. It is not restricted to sermons starting from a biblical text.

In Theses 5 and 10 we indicated the care taken by Jesus in his preaching to begin with the known in order to lead his hearers to the unknown, and to take account of what they know and what they are.

The example of Jesus and the apostles shows that the point of departure for preaching is sought sometimes in the traditional culture (whether of the Old Testament or some other) and sometimes in recent events or daily life.

In other words, the preaching of the good news is not limited to sermons starting from some biblical text.

According to Luke 4: 16-21, Jesus at times made a sermon on a biblical text. Elsewhere, however, he introduced his message without reference to a text, often making use of some event, or some question put to him, as an opportunity for preaching. Similarly Peter begins with a text from the Old Testament in Acts 2: 14-36, while on another occasion he uses as his opportunity popular excitement over the healing of the lame man at the Gate Beautiful (Acts 3: 12-26).

Paul at Lystra (Acts 14: 8-18) starts (as in Romans 1: 20) from God's revelation in creation and providence (v. 17). At Athens he takes his theme from the religious life and literature of the people there (Acts 17: 16-23).

Thus, when the hearer is Jewish, familiar with the Law and the Prophets, preaching starts from this knowledge and uses a biblical text. When the hearer is a Gentile, unfamiliar with the biblical tradition, preaching seeks another point of departure, in things with which the hearer is concerned.

If we accept the view taken by J.-J. Leuba in his article on 'Doctrine' in *Vocabulaire biblique,* we shall have to say that preaching, the moment it ceases to have a Jewish audience, differs from teaching precisely in dispensing with scriptural references, of which teaching stands in need. 'Founded on Holy Scripture, which it is commissioned to explain, the teaching ministry has this specific difference from the preaching of the Gospel message. Sometimes Jesus preaches, sometimes he teaches. The two verbs, associated in Matthew 11: 1, are not tautological (any more than in Acts, at numerous places). When Jesus or the apostles preach, they announce the Gospel, the unprecedented "news" that the Kingdom of God has come and is present in Jesus Christ. Scripture plays no decisive rôle here. But when they teach, Jesus and the apostles begin with Scripture, and demonstrate how present facts correspond with the sacred history of Israel and reveal its full meaning and richness. . . . From then on, the Old and New Testaments will constitute the unique source of all Christian teaching.'

Leuba points out that two-thirds of the New Testament passages containing the verb 'to teach' occur in the Gospels and the first part of Acts. 'The teaching could be directly addressed only to Jews. For the Gentiles, preaching was necessary in order to lead them to Christ, and only then could all the richness of this same Christ be shown to them in the Scriptures . . . Christian teaching could be addressed only to those already led to faith by the preaching.'[14]

The movement by which preaching goes physically to encounter men, in order to win them as disciples, and the movement by which it goes spiritually to meet their aspirations and the things that they already know (just like the parable, which seeks among the realities familiar to its audience the illustration calculated to illuminate a truth of which they have no inkling) justifies the frequently used metaphor that describes preaching as 'fishing for men'. The preacher must leave his home to go to look for the fish. He must cast his line far out, after first baiting the hook with something calculated to attract the fish, something suited to its tastes, needs and habits. Then, once the fish is hooked, he must draw it towards him and snatch it from its natural habitat. The process of being denaturalized must be no light matter for the fish subjected to its first flight through the air!

THESIS 17

The preaching of Jesus also contributes indirectly to the instruction of the disciples through the reactions provoked by its polemical character. Changed from an announcement into denouncement, preaching looks to stirring up the anger which will destroy it, and whose flame will enable Jesus to forge his Church as a sword for the conquest of the world.

All the threads of our argument draw together here. As we have said, Jesus went to meet the aspirations of the people, by healing the sick and feeding the hungry; then he withdrew. His withdrawal was intended, as we have seen, to constrain genuinely interested hearers to follow him, to transform their aspirations, to lead them to understand that what they suffered from most was not lack of bread, nor was their heaviest burden the dominion of Rome. But this withdrawal had another effect, and undoubtedly another intention: 'I came to cast fire upon the earth,' said Jesus. The context, 'I came to bring not peace but a sword,' helps us to see that by the fire is meant the anger of the people. Jesus lit this fire in the hearts of those he healed and then left still a prey to disease, of those he fed and then left still to toil and hunger, of those he gathered together, aroused, compromised and then refused to lead in the fight to liberate their country. Jesus kindled these desires, fed and strengthened them with temporary satisfactions. His withdrawal left a sudden vacuum. Disillusion exploded in anger. From then onwards, like a good blacksmith, Jesus fed the flame. His preaching became polemical, offensive, insulting: 'Hypocrites, blind, adulterous and sinful generation, unbelieving and perverse nation, whited sepulchres, robbers, children of Gehenna, children of the devil, serpents, vipers, liars, murderers.' Jesus knew full well the storm he was bringing down upon himself. He needed the fire of this wrath for the forging of his sword, the Church. Our brittle hearts, at once too hard and too soft, fluid and yet unyielding, lacking suppleness, tenderness and firmness, are poor material, requiring purification, needing to be melted down and hammered. Hard work! In the fire of popular anger, all that personal ambition, political passion and love of glory which, mingled in the souls of the disciples with their passion for justice, had attracted them to him, will be consumed. Finally when every-thing is ready, the flame must be brought to a sufficient heat to separate the element of excessive self-esteem, the root principle of our human frailty, from the element of humble and legitimate self-love. In the hour of wrath, the disciples forsake and deny their master. From then on, each knows his own and other men's vanity. Every illusion as to his own merit or others' esteem for him goes up in smoke; God alone becomes his confidence. After the fire, the wind will disperse the ashes of pride, and lay bare the rock of faith on which the Church is to be built.

Because the disciples have been not only hearers, and then transmitters and associates of the preaching of Jesus, but also its victims, they will be able to carry it on.

Part Two

PREACHING IN CONTEMPORARY PRACTICE

Having analysed some of the characteristics of Jesus' preaching and teaching, and of that of the apostles, we shall be brief in our treatment of our contemporary witness and service. There is indeed little to be said about our preaching, since we have none, or at most only vestiges. Still, that at least had to be said, for we believe that we have. And that is a serious illusion.

We speak often and wisely (Mathiot, Barth) about preaching. But by 'preaching' we commonly mean the sermon, the homily delivered in church during worship, and addressed to a Christian congregation. By a 'preacher' we mean a specialist, usually paid but sometimes voluntary, who provides this kind of discourse. In short, by a misuse of words the enormity of which is disguised by long custom and inertia, we identify this 'preaching' in church to a Christian congregation with the Church's preaching to the world, i.e. that which the Church is commissioned to address to those who do not belong to it. Hence our next thesis:

THESIS 18

Whatever other purpose the Sunday sermon may serve, it usurps the function of preaching without fulfilling it, and lacks the essential characteristics of preaching.

The Sunday sermon is not addressed to the crowd, to the people, but to those we call the 'faithful', whom it might be more accurate sometimes to call the *'habitués'* or sermon-tasters.[15] Most of our contemporaries forgather and meet in places other than our churches. What is said in church, therefore, whatever other interest it may have, does not reach them. The Sunday sermon, which we call 'preaching', is in fact restricted to a few.

Not only does the Sunday sermon lack the unrestricted openness of preaching, it also lacks—and the two things are related—the itinerant character of preaching. The 'preacher' does not move on.

He reiterates instead of itinerating.[16] The same sermon-maker, in the same place, replenishes the same hearers week after week, year in year out. Several consequences flow from this situation.

First and most obviously, the good news, the promise and demand of the Gospel, is not taken to the people—at any rate, not by the sermon. The people do not receive what is due to them; the Church thus fails in its mission. This mission remains unfulfilled, at least as far as the sermon goes.

Secondly, the sermon-maker addressing himself as he does to a group of *habitués,* takes little trouble to inform himself about the aspirations of the people, or to link his discourse thereon. He is consequently unable to interest them, when by chance they do come to hear him.

Similarly, the sermon, since it does not deal with the questions and objections of the ordinary people whom it ignores, and has no need to direct into the right channels the enthusiasm of the converts it does not make, or to face persecution from those it does not provoke, is not stimulated either to renewal or radical change. It simply repeats itself, goes round and round in a circle, itself falls asleep and sends others to sleep!

Finally, concentrating on these *habitués,* the sermon fails to associate them with the task of preaching. It not only fails to carry this out itself, but also, through encouraging the illusion that it does, excuses and turns away from it those whom it should mobilize for carrying it out.

Indeed, the 'faithful' in general share in neither the preparation, nor criticism, nor furtherance of the preaching. By a radical perversion, they have become merely the recipients of preaching, and no longer those who relay it.

The Sunday sermon is an illusory substitute for preaching. The Church which tolerates this situation might be compared with a farmer who stayed at home and sowed his seed in the drawing room rather than venture out into the fields, which he abandons to proliferate with every kind of noxious weed. The sermon-maker and his *habitués* while imagining that they are giving and receiving the Church's preaching, are guilty in fact of spiritual onanism, and of withholding their seed from those to whom they owe it.

The Sunday sermon will lack purpose and never recover its meaning until it is understood by all as an instrument for the instruction of disciples. Rightly understood, the sermon is part of the Church's teaching ministry, an instrument for the explication and demonstration of Scripture. It has also an exhortatory purpose (*paraclesis*) which in some respects approximates to preaching.[17] It is important however to subordinate the sermon both to preaching and to service, since it is not intended merely to exhort the faithful to live better lives but to serve and to witness more effectively. It is intended to prepare the assembled disciples to engage in the work of preaching. It is intended to prepare with them the Church's preaching to the people, as the task of the Church when it is dispersed in the world, dissolved like salt in the soup, every day of the week.[18]

THESIS 19

The deterioration of preaching is accompanied by a deterioration in teaching.

Again our analysis must begin with the fact that when the sermon is taken as a substitute for preaching, the itinerant character of preaching is lost. Suppose (and it does happen) that the sermon-maker faithfully communicates in his sermon the message of Christ the King and the summons to conversion. Suppose some new hearer, one not inoculated against the Gospel, has been led by chance or curiosity, or even let us say by Providence, to hear him. Suppose this hearer to be moved by the faithful proclamation of God's gifts and promises. It is now the moment to invite him to make his decision. The sermon-maker will not omit to do this. He will occasionally acquit himself with eloquence, urging his hearer to 'give his life to Christ', to 'renounce sin'. He will even insist very properly on the urgency of this decision, as radical as it is unfortunately vague. 'Today,' he will say, 'choose life!' But his practice soon gives the lie to his words, sometimes to his hearer's embarrassment, sometimes to his relief. Just because the exhortation he has heard is so vague, the hearer cannot see clearly exactly what step he is being asked to take. He may, moreover, quite naturally hesitate to believe, to commit his whole life. This is so important, it demands reflection. However, there is in fact no call for any hasty decision, whatever may be said to the contrary, since the 'preacher' has renounced his itinerancy. Everyone knows he will be back again next week, and the week after, in the same place, offering the same exhortations and the same prospects to the same hearers, playing over and over again, Sunday by Sunday, the same great scene: 'Today, choose life!' without apparently ever suspecting that the very repetition of this theme cancels its effect. The interested but cautious hearer would be foolish to take any risk (exactly what risk, anyway?) without more information. Certain of having another opportunity, he sees no urgent necessity to make a decision for which he feels unprepared, despite all the eloquence— a decision which he will certainly not take, once he has become hardened to such appeals. He settles down in this state of indecision, which has every chance of becoming permanent and fatal. At best he will himself become an *habitué,* an *aficionado,* a regular attender admiring in amateur fashion the subtleties of the sermon and the eloquence of the 'preacher', but never imagining himself called to come down into the arena.

Our church members, deprived as they are of any responsibility for the Church's preaching, are thus robbed of an indispensable means of instruction and of the deepening of their faith. Instead of 'living' in Christ, they vegetate, atrophy, and become sterile, unfruitful branches. Having nothing to pass on, they have no desire to receive anything. Their personal stagnation inevitably results in a stagnant church. Arrested growth in the individual has its counterpart in the arrested growth and development of the church, numerically and spiritually.

Not that the minister does not think of himself as a teacher. Yet his teaching is often abstract and remote, designed to enrich leisure moments, but demanding no real sacrifice of time or habit on the part of its recipients. It fails to draw people out from their accustomed ways; it is not bound up with activity thought out, undertaken and directed by a group. We listen to it, but are not constrained or helped to express in word and action the new thoughts and feelings which it claims to suggest and develop in us. A strange business, self-condemned to impotence!

It is, moreover, a teaching directed to and reaching only children and adolescents. It comes to an end—in most cases for life—before adult years are attained. Contrast this with secular studies, which tend nowadays, for an increasing number of young people (including our catechumens) to go on much longer, with the enrichment that education brings plus the dangers of a half-baked culture. Then, experience of life, of military service and war, of work in some industry or profession, of trade unions, of political, conjugal and family responsibilities, begins to superimpose its own practical and unconscious lessons on the lessons learnt in Sunday school and communicants' class. How many of those who have finished receiving instruction are there strong enough to cope with the school of life unharmed? How many have grasped the vital necessity of continuing their spiritual growth and education beyond their first communion? How many ministers who preach the 'new birth' pay any attention to the 'new growth'? How many ministers, instead of repeating every year or two the same course of instruction, continue to go deeper in teaching those who passed through their hands earlier, and make use of them to instruct the beginners —the only real way of bringing up catechumens to become catechists, and of fully meeting their real needs?

By confining its teaching more and more to children, and neglecting the education of adults, the Church is conforming itself to the world's fashion. For almost a century schools have provided children with a theoretical education as a prelude to life and its responsibilities, on the assumption that it is the child who has to be educated, and that the adult must then live on the capital acquired in childhood. In fact this is the devil's way of stifling man's growth and arresting it, through pride or despair, at an immature stage of development. The Church, however, instructed in the freedom and continuous growth given to men in Jesus Christ, cannot accept this notion of an education that is confined to one period of human life, and divorced from practical obedience and the expression of what is learned.

THESIS 20

The deterioration of preaching and teaching is accompanied by a deterioration in service.

As a result of the immobility of preaching and teaching, church members eager to express their faith and serve their neighbours, but lacking the gifts of speech necessary for the work of the full-time ministry (which claims a virtual monopoly of the oral forms of witness), are left with no other outlet but charitable works. Much enthusiastic and intelligent service of God and man goes into these works of mercy. A good deal of devotion is invested in them. But the impoverishment of preaching and teaching carries with it serious weaknesses in this area too.

Just as the sermon, when it usurps the place of preaching, all too often turns the Church narcissistically in upon itself, so that it preaches the Gospel to itself instead of to the world and in the world, so too the Church's works of mercy (often carried out by the diaconates in congregations) are often confined to giving assistance to its own members. This certainly is necessary and laudable, and may even be assigned a certain priority, since mutual love is a sign of that which the preaching proclaims. But the service of the poor, who are mostly strangers to our churches, is forgotten. Service, though here not entirely divorced from preaching, is nevertheless also a victim of the narcissistic perversion of churches which reserve the benefits of preaching for their own members.

Other charitable organizations throw themselves courageously into the work of serving those in need without distinction of race or religion. But the leaders or officials of these organizations lay themselves open to the charge of neglecting to explain by the spoken word the meaning of the service they render. This may be due to their fear of seeming to be merely propagandists for some ecclesiastical institution, or to the fact that they have become chary of the merely spoken word, through the bankruptcy of teaching and the taking over of preaching by the professional ministry.

Enterprises initiated under the constraint of Christian love, and for greater effectiveness given institutional form and run by lay people, come in time to be absorbed into the necessary welfare services through which the civil community cares for itself. Such good works are of course still needed—hospitals, schools, orphanages, etc.—and the activity and witness of alert Christians within them preserve their significance. Yet they no longer give more than a very indirect and attenuated witness to the Gospel; they no longer clearly represent the Church's engagement in the world.

Finally, the Church's tolerance of the stagnation of its adult membership and its own organizations, the absence within the Church itself of any system of continuous education and constant renewal of Christian understanding, make it easy for the Church and its charitable institutions to settle down and go to sleep in their routine ways. Instead of multiplying, and recognizing the signs of the Kingdom of him who makes all things new, instead of remaining responsive and inventive, alert to the fresh needs and new aspirations of men, instead of letting themselves be renewed by the conversation which they ought to keep going between the world and God, the churches and their charitable organizations are too often preoccupied with self-preservation. From time to time, constrained by the impatience of love and weary of ecclesiastical routines and mediocrities, pioneers establish on the frontiers of church institutions new movements and enterprises which answer needs the churches have not discerned, and in which the Church's witness and service are expressed outside the churches. But in this way, these movements and enterprises draw away out of traditional church circles the most generous, courageous, and impatient of Christian believers, often leaving the direction of church institutions to the less daring and creative members, thus aggravating the immobility of the Church. The new movements or organizations, which at first seemed to carry all the Church's hopes, by their separation from the deep, hidden life of the Church become institutionalized in turn, concealing their own original springs and, because no longer subjected to questioning by the Word, ceasing to be continually renewed in their thinking.

Towards a Conclusion!

I have been reproached—quite fairly, as it seems to me—with having limited the foregoing analysis to the purely formal characteristics of preaching. My reason was simply the conviction that it was here that our 'preaching' differed from that of Jesus and the apostles. So far as content was concerned, I assumed agreement: salvation by faith; the sovereignty of grace; the love of God; reconciliation.

But I have come to ask myself whether our infidelity in the matter of form does not in fact affect the actual content of preaching. It would need another book to deal with that subject. Here we may simply put a few questions.

Can we reform our theory and practice of preaching, and recover the forms of the preaching, teaching and service characteristic of the life of Jesus and the apostles, without challenging the very basis of our contemporary preaching? To be more specific, if Jesus' preaching was itinerant, victorious, and universal in scope, if it was expressed in service to the point of sacrifice, was this not because it announced the nearness, the imminence of the Kingdom of God?

And if our preaching is muted, evasive, and lacking fire, if it is often accompanied by a service which costs us no more than we can easily spare, is this not because we have ceased to proclaim the imminent Kingdom?

Can we recover today the certainty of the imminence of the Kingdom, which is the content of a confident and victorious preaching, and with it, its driving power?

Postscript

(Reporting on discussion at the Synod meeting)

Some questioned any comparison between Jesus' preaching and ours in principle. Jesus is divine, we are human, the circumstances were different, etc. But was he not fully human, like us in all points? Did he not send us 'as the Father sent me'?

Some thought my address was too polemical. I was clearly out to 'smash everything'. But what I was trying to do was to 'look at Jesus', as faith directs us to do, and to search the Scriptures, as the Reformation bade.

Regret was expressed that so little reference was made to the Holy Spirit, without whose power all our efforts are vain. But is this not what we look to the Spirit to enable us to do, to look to Jesus and to change us stage by stage into his likeness?

Others said I have over-emphasized what the Church does (its mission), at the expense of what it is. The worship of God preceding and accompanying preaching, the practical expression of love between brethren, are of the Church's essence and in themselves constitute a testimony which some would regard as in the last resort sufficient. But does the Church enjoy a monopoly of praise and service? Surely what is peculiar to the Church is its commission to proclaim the Kingdom of the Son of man? Is not this its *raison d'être*?

Some reproached me with failing to speak of the sacraments and their preaching function. It is true that in the Lord's Supper we proclaim the Lord's death until he come. I also believe that reflection on the Lord's Supper will clarify the question, raised in several groups, of the distinction between a national Church and the congregation of believers. Does the New Testament know of any other Church than the church of believers? One group said that Jesus did not tell all those whom he converted to move off. But did those who did not move off really share in that enterprise of spreading the Gospel, which is called the Church?

The idea of growing in Christ was questioned. 'To be really born anew each day would mean to receive everything, **not** to develop and grow.' Certainly we cannot be born and grow in Christ without grace. It is right to emphasize this dependence on grace. We cannot, however, eliminate the idea of growth without distorting the teaching of the New Testament and failing to do justice to the action of grace.

The above reactions and objections made in the Synod are those which merited consideration and reply. They do not represent the view of the Synod, of course, any more than my own theses do. Other reactions explicitly endorsed and other suggestions offered implicitly approved the intention of seeking in Jesus our example, of taking fresh hold of and of giving expression to the universal priesthood of believers, and of restoring to preaching a greater mobility, and of developing ways of continuing education for our church members.

NOTES

In support of this thesis I originally intended to cite the similarity between preaching and the parables, assuming that the parable, according to Mark 4 and parallels, was intentionally enigmatic, its explanation being reserved for the disciples only and withheld from the crowd. A reading of Masson's *Les paraboles de Marc* 4 (Delachaux et Niestlé, Lausanne, 1945) showed this to be an untenable argument. Masson questions, correctly it would seem, Mark's interpretation of Jesus' use of parables.

Verses 10 and 11, describing a conversation with the Twelve, are arbitrarily inserted at this point. It seems better, moreover, to translate 'everything comes' (Stapfer) or 'everything happens in parables' (Segond, Pernot), rather than 'everything is presented' (Synodal, Goguel) or 'everything is announced' (Crampon) in parables. For the reference here is not to speaking in parables, but to the acts of Jesus, which are a mystery revealed to the disciples, but, to those outside, 'parables' the point of which escapes them (Cf. Heb. 9 : 9; 11 : 19. This interpretation of Mark 4 is supported by Lohmeyer. Cf. the LXX version of Deut. 28 : 37).

Masson regards vv. 12 and 34 as editorial additions which puzzled Matthew and Luke. The parables have become obscure for us; without their original context their point is lost. Mark regarded this obscurity as intentional, but this is contrary to the Gospel tradition, for which the parable illustrates the teaching and makes it easier for the simple to understand. Mark's interpretation resulted from theological reflection in which the supposedly intentional obscurity of the parable was linked up with Israel's hardening of heart.

The distinction I draw here between preaching and teaching has been made by scholars. Thus Chr. Senft in his article 'Prêcher' in *Vocabulaire biblique* (Delachaux et Niestlé, 1954) writes : 'The verbs "preach" and "announce" are an imperfect translation of the Greek words. "Preach", in particular, has lost for us its original sense. It now suggests a more or less personal and individual, more or less doctrinal and theoretical discourse addressed to a closed group of believers within the confines of a church building. This is exactly the opposite of the idea it was originally intended to, and did in fact, express, namely, the proclamation made by a herald or town crier, following the ear-splitting sound of a trumpet out in the open in full light of day.'

NOTE 2 (*page* 9)

The Rev. J. Deransart suggests we reread the section on 'The Destiny of the Elect' in Barth's *Church Dogmatics* II, 2, from which we extract the following passage (p. 439 of the French translation):
'The existence of the apostolate actually begins with the activity of Jesus himself. . . . In calling these men to him, Jesus does not promise to make Christians of them, and then apostles; he promises right away that he will make them fishers of men, that is, apostles, bearers of a commission to be given to them; they are to seek and gather men as a fisherman seeks and gathers fish. If from that moment, and on the basis of this calling, they are called his *mathētai* (disciples), that indicates that what he has to teach and what they have to learn from him is not some private way to their own salvation and blessedness; before all else they have to understand the message which they are to carry among men, in order to seek and gather them. What is involved is a calling, in the literal sense of that word. Jesus takes them from their own line of business, or rather he gives them a new one. . . . It is to learn their new calling . . . that the fishers of Galilee leave their nets and boats to follow him. . . . He has chosen them to give them this new calling. . . . The individual is elected by Jesus in order to belong to him and to do what Jesus himself has been elect to do, to preach the Gospel to many.'

NOTE 3 (*page* 10)

It will be noticed that the geographical and cultural displacement caused by preaching necessarily has a temporal dimension as well, and that its movement can also be studied from this standpoint. Jesus invites his people to discern the signs of the times, to know when the harvest is ripe, to recognize and seize the key moments, the propitious opportunities, the *kairoi* which occur in the life of an individual, of a group, or of a people, and make certain things possible for them.

Let us note (anticipating what will be said later about our contemporary practice of preaching) what Roger Mehl recently wrote in his article on 'L'Eglise de l'Avenir' (in *Revue de l'Evangélisation*, No. 98, Nov.-Dec., 1961). He makes the same connection between physical mobility and intellectual openness, as regards the Church of the future, as that which we see as characteristic of the practice of Jesus and the apostles. 'Churches no longer dominate cities. Their very immobility has resulted in their isolation. The Church of tomorrow will be *a Church on the move*; it will go to rejoin men where they live, in the places where they work, in their family circles, and just as much in the places where they spend their leisure. . . . *Mobility is essential*

for encounter with our fellow-men, for it is only in encounter with
other people that the Gospel becomes a power for life. . . . Again it is
a question of meeting men *amid their problems* . . . the problems with
which our fellow-man has to cope, the problem of being reconciled to
his wife, of providing his children with a good education, of the proper
way of tackling his work and of seeking some meaning to give it, the
problem of politics and of political struggles. . . .'

NOTE 4 (*page* 13)

We cannot dogmatize in a general way that the only response to the call
to repentance or the only way of salvation is to become a disciple and
to follow Jesus. Some may do God's will and love him in their brethren
without realizing it (Mt. 25). Election concerns some, so that salvation
may be offered to all. It was Jesus who chose his intimate disciples, not
they who chose him. Yet he emphasized the impossibility of being his
disciple without following him on his perilous journey, and he asked
men to count the cost (cf. Lk. 9 : 57-62 : 'No man, having put his hand
to the plough, and looking back, is fit for the kingdom of God').

We quote from Karl Barth again (op. cit. II, 2, p. 411): 'Each elect
individual is, as such, a messenger of God. . . . This is his service and
his mission. He is called to become himself a herald, to keep the call
going in the ears of the world. . . . The Twelve were *called to follow*
Jesus, so that they might *put themselves on the road,* as disciples of
Jesus, to go among all the nations, and to go before the nations, in
order thus to summon them to follow Jesus.' Cf. the sending of the
disciple in Mk. 5 : 18-20.

NOTE 5 (*page* 13)

There are thus two kinds of familiarity. One is creative, established
between teacher and pupil in the course of their walks together, born
in the expectancy and the creation of a common future, nourished by
the exciting experience of growth together. The other is at bottom only
habit, which, imagining that it can make do with a general impression
of what people are, by its very nature stifles development; it is this
which causes a prophet to be unhonoured in his own country. It is
with this later kind of familiarity that a break must be made in favour
of the former.

NOTE 6 (*page* 13)

M. Philibert, 'In favour of an intelligent Church', *Secretary,* 1961, No. 2.
Cf. P. Bonnard, 'Le Discernement de la volonté de Dieu dans le

Christianisme primitif', in *Communauté des Disséminés,* No. 10, Dec., 1960, and in *Christianisme Social,* Jan.-Feb., 1961. André de Robert, 'Discerner la volonté de Dieu', *Bulletin de Villemétrie,* April, 1961 : 'Le renouvellement de l'intelligence', ibid. Aug., 1961, Sept., 1961.

NOTE 7 *(page 14)*

I follow here a French version (Segond) which translates : 'et croissant *par* la connaissance de Dieu'. There are several variants of the Greek text.

NOTE 8 *(page 17)*

Cf. article 'Prêcher' in *Vocabulaire biblique* : 'Preaching is accompanied by miracles, healings and especially exorcisms. They are not two parallel activities, but two inseparable aspects of the same event : the Kingdom comes, and the bonds which enslave men begin to fall off. The words of Jesus are not simply teaching, but the proclamation of a fact, the fact of God's decisive intervention in history.' Cf. II Cor. 4 : 6 : 'Seeing it is God, that said, Light shall shine out of darkness, who shined in our hearts, to give the light of the knowledge of the glory of God in the face of Jesus Christ.'

NOTE 9 *(page 22)*

Cf. article 'Prêcher' : in *Vocabulaire biblique,* 'The Kingdom of God is not something distinct from Jesus Christ. It is in him that it comes and must be recognized. . . . In St John's Gospel, Jesus himself is seen as the only theme of the preaching.'

NOTE 10 *(page 24)*

Cf. Michel Bouttier, 'Comment l'Eglise doit-elle parler au monde d'aujourd'hui?' in *Christianisme Social,* Sept-Oct., 1948 : 'The whole of Scripture reminds us that the essential function of the preaching of God's Word is to provoke division and decision. It is a sharp two-edged sword, a sign to be spoken against, which creates division among men. Some receive it with a joyous faith, others reject it, and not only reject it but persecute its prophets.'

NOTE 11 *(page 24)*

Cf. Karl Barth, op. cit. II, 2, pp. 439f. 'In choosing and calling his disciples, Jesus intends that they shall actively work with him, and share with him in his own ministry. And this ministry is the prophetic

office. The other participants of the Gospel witness are there to show
that they cannot share in this ministry without sharing in the sufferings
and the glory of Jesus—and certainly also that Jesus is not only the
prophet, but also the priest and king.'

NOTE 12 (*page* 26)

Essay published by Kierkegaard in 1847 under the initials 'H.H.', made
available in French by the translator (Tisseau) in 1935 in the Dept. of
Vendée.

NOTE 13 (*page* 29)

Cf. Acts 4 : 13—'When they saw the boldness of Peter and John, they
were astonished, knowing that they were unlettered men.'

NOTE 14 (*page* 35)†

A short pamphlet has been published in French by Delachaux et Niestlé
entitled *La proclamation de l'Evangile* (an English translation of this
is to be published this year by the Westminster Press, Philadelphia,
under the title *The Preaching of the Gospel*). This appears as an essay
by Karl Barth, but is actually an adaptation made from ancient notes
by a student who attended a lecture by Barth on this topic. The long
note I originally wrote at this point discussed the thesis of this pamphlet.
I agreed with Barth's statement that, in preaching, we bear positive
witness to revelation. I disagreed, however, with Barth, or perhaps it
was his adapter, who argued that, to be positive, preaching had to be
an exposition of Scripture. Naturally I admit that the substance of
preaching must be derived from Scripture. But this does not mean that
formally it must start from and be an exposition of a biblical text.
Some have insisted that my criticism did not apply to Barth's own
position, and that Barth explicitly states in *Church Dogmatics* that the
ecclesiastical character of preaching does not necessarily mean that it
must formally start from a biblical text. These friends did me too much
honour, in thinking that my criticisms might shake, or even spoil, the
powerful castle of the *Dogmatik* which I had no intention whatever
of attacking! I still adhere, nevertheless, to everything which I originally
wrote in my French note here. But I am quite ready to suppose that
my criticisms applied in part not to Barth's own meaning, but to a
rather poor and ambiguous adaptation. Since the English reader has

†This is a new note by Prof. Philibert, instead of an English
translation of the extended note which stands in the French text.—Ed.

hitherto had no occasion to be misled by such an adaptation, the discussion of it can be of no interest for him.

We maintain, whatever Barth has said or intended to say, there or elsewhere, that preaching in the sense of the New Testament is not done by the Sunday sermon delivered to the Christian community. We are not prepared to agree with the statement that 'preaching is only possible within the Church', that 'it must be recognized that those who heard preaching were baptized men and women'. We think that Peter's Pentecostal sermon (Acts 2), which led to the baptism of three thousand persons, was not addressed to baptized persons, yet was indeed preaching. We are even prepared to assert that Paul's speech to the Athenians was preaching, and that was certainly not an exposition within the Church of a biblical text. I know that this statement of mine may arouse a still greater fuss. Nevertheless I maintain that the testimony of one man inside the Church (in its building and to a Christian congregation) does not constitute preaching. It is simply part of the instruction given to the disciples, who have come to be taught, and who ought then to go out to preach.

NOTE 15 (*page* 38)

Cf. Michel Bouttier art. cit. 'People nowadays are, as it were, inoculated, and the Church's preaching is surrounded by general indifference.' Etienne Mathiot, art. cit., regards contemporary preaching as a 'monologue which cannot but produce hearers who are irresponsible and in some way weak'.

NOTE 16 (*page* 39)

Michel Bouttier, ibid. 'The centuries have made of us imitators, not prophets.'

NOTE 17 (*page* 40)

In 'La Transmission de l'évangile' (*Etudes théologiques et religieuses,* No. 2, Montpellier, 1957), Ferrier-Welty insists on the distinction between teaching (*didascalia*) and exhortation (*paraclesis*). In our view, teaching can and should include an element of exhortation, in order to give it personal application. But Ferrier-Welty, misled by the traditional usage of the word 'preaching' (which we reject), uses expressions which are ambiguous. Sometimes he happily notes the subordination of paraclesis to the preaching which will be the task of the hearers. Paraclesis, he says, represents 'this personal quality of any

54 CHRIST'S PREACHING—AND OURS

addressed by one man to another with a view to his strengthening and
consecration *in the apostolic task.*' 'The chief point on which Paul
dwells,' says Calvin, 'is to confirm Timothy not only in the faith of
the Gospel, but also in *the constant and pure preaching of the Gospel.*'
But sometimes Ferrier-Welty incorrectly omits from his definition of
paraclesis this reference to preaching, which Calvin explicitly makes.
'Paraclesis is itself preaching, in so far as it is the word of the Gospel
addressed personally by one believer to one or more other believers,
with a view to their growth in faith and obedience to the faith.' For
Calvin, as we saw, paraclesis is confirmation rather than proclamation,
a first step towards preaching.

Later on, Ferrier-Welty recovers the essential element omitted from
his definition, and rightly declares : 'Preaching is that for which the
ministry is established. The aim of the ministry is that the Gospel may
be proclaimed. The aim of preaching the Gospel is preaching itself. . . .
Preaching is done that the task of preaching may be carried on. The
preaching of the Gospel is the goal of the ministry since its aim is to
fashion preachers, men apt to teach and to exhort.' Unfortunately in
what follows Ferrier-Welty succumbs to current clericalism, and reserves
the exercise of the preaching ministry and the title of servant of the
Lord to some Christians only. He recovers a sound line regarding
exhortation, however, when he states : 'Paraclesis does not define a
particular mode of life, any more than it provides the rough draft of
a Christian ethic. It refers entirely to the transmission of the message.'

Allowing, then, that the Sunday sermon addressed to believers has
an exhortatory aspect, this element is much more an aspect of teaching
than a supplement to it. Teaching is personal, not general; practical,
and not only theoretical. Ferrier-Welty says he wishes to distinguish
teaching from exhortation, not in order to separate them, but to unite
them more closely. Having emphasized the oral and personal character
of didascalia, he specifically says : 'In the pair of words didascalia-
paraclesis, the second term adds nothing to the first, but simply gives
its exact force.'

NOTE 18 (*page* 40)

Not merely does the 'preacher' no longer 'move on', he no longer dies!
He dies no more, and his hearers, his disciples, are consequently faced
no longer with the need to replace him. They rest themselves in him.
He provides them with an alibi. He does not make them face the
question of quitting their family and their job, to go to spread the
Gospel. This preacher no longer dies, because progress in comfort,
hygiene and medicine has raised the standard and increased the

expectation of life. The preacher also no longer dies because he no longer disturbs anyone. No one would think of trying to silence him, since he speaks into the wind. No one thinks of removing his sword, for in his hands the sword of the Spirit has become a toy which does not frighten even children.

Michel Bouttier (art. cit.): 'Let us not deceive ourselves. We are afraid of this incarnation of the Word, which is the very gift of power of the Spirit. The true prophet is vulnerable; he is always caught. The message he carries places his life in jeopardy. . . . Men will heed only those who put their whole future into what they say, their wealth, their position, their flesh and their blood. . . . Deprived of this incarnation, the preaching of the Gospel is prisoner of a traditional form. It is cut off from the language of the day. It is instructive to note, says A. de Robert, how the forms of the Gospel message have been moulded by forms derived from the lecture theatre, the public platform, the sermon, and not from ordinary conversation. The consequence is that the content of the Gospel, deprived of its traditional form, of its mould, becomes incommunicable. People may at a pinch receive it, but they will not pass it on.

'When our preaching no longer specializes in heavenly and eternal things, when it again faces the problems of the hour, when we no longer speak down from the height of the pulpit and in a robe, when we speak with men face to face, as man to man, when our preaching ceases to be the exclusive business of the preacher and becomes the responsibility of the congregation itself, then we shall rediscover the secret of extending the Christian faith.'